This library edition published in 2012 by Walter Foster Publishing, Inc.
Distributed by Black Rabbit Books.
P.O. Box 3263 Mankato, Minnesota 56002

Designed and published by Walter Foster Publishing, Inc.
Walter Foster is a registered trademark.

Printed in Mankato, Minnesota, USA by CG Book Printers, a division of Corporate Graphics.

First Library Edition

Library of Congress Cataloging-in-Publication Data

Winterberg, Jenna.
   Watch me draw favorite pets / story by Jenna Winterberg ; illustrations by Diana Fisher. -- First Library Edition.
       pages cm
   ISBN 978-1-936309-77-1
   1. Animals in art--Juvenile literature. 2. Drawing--Technique--Juvenile literature. I. Fisher, Diana, illustrator.
II. Title.
   NC783.8.P48W56 2012
   743.6--dc23
                                2012004729

052012
17679

9 8 7 6 5 4 3 2 1

Favorite Pets

Story by Jenna Winterberg • Illustrations by Diana Fisher

Walter Foster

Meet Boomer. Boomer lives with the Bailey family. The Baileys give him a lot of love and attention. They feed him, walk him, and pet him regularly. The Baileys also play games with Boomer, and Boomer watches over the whole Bailey household. It's a dog's life, and Boomer loves it!

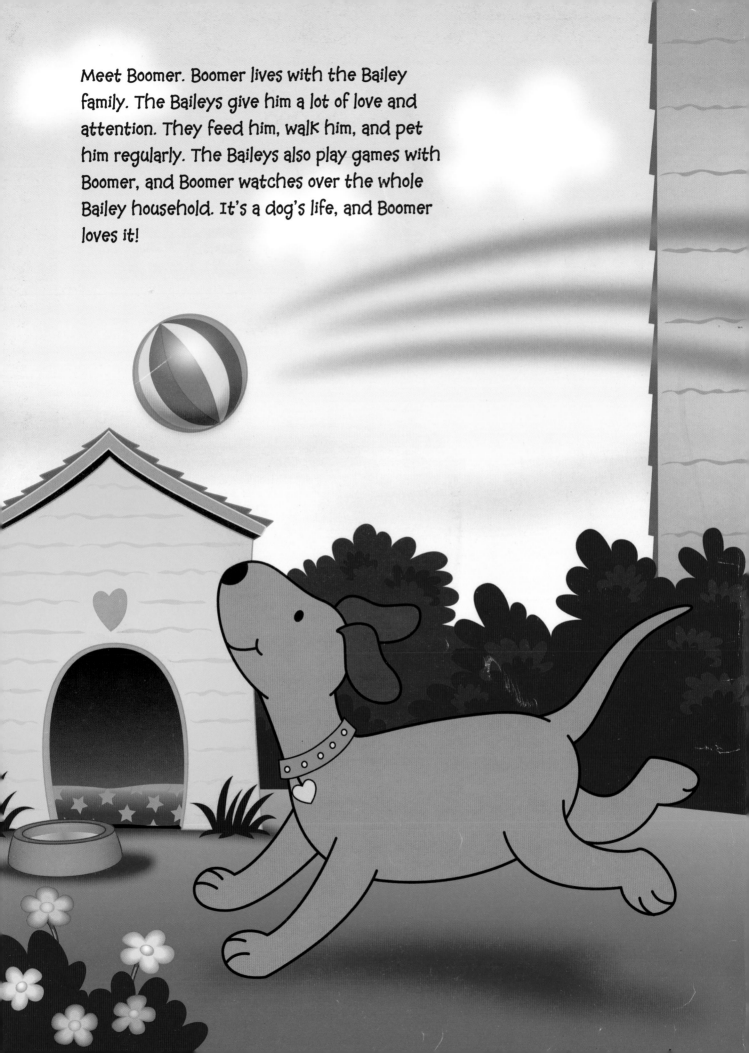

Draw Boomer the dog!

1

2

3

4

5

6

Boomer's best friend is a kitten named Mew. Mew is very young, so she doesn't know the rules of the house yet. For example, she climbs on the kitchen counters and naps on Mr. Bailey's favorite chair! But because Mew is Boomer's best friend, he never tattles. When the Baileys find fur in all the wrong places, they blame Boomer. "BOO-MER!"

Draw Mew the Kitten!

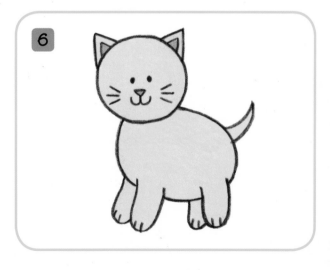

Mew is very fond of Gilbert, another member of the Bailey family. But Mew doesn't want to make friends with Gil—she would like nothing better than to eat the little fish! So Boomer carefully watches over Gil to make sure he is safe, which means that Boomer is there to take the blame when Mr. Bailey discovers the water Mew spilled. "BOO-MER!"

Draw Gilbert the fish!

1

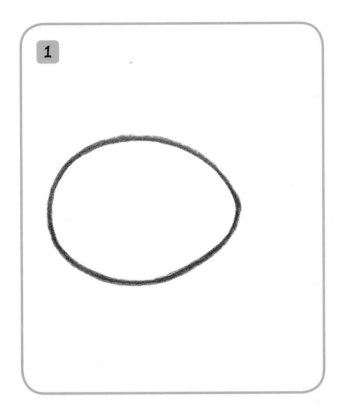

2

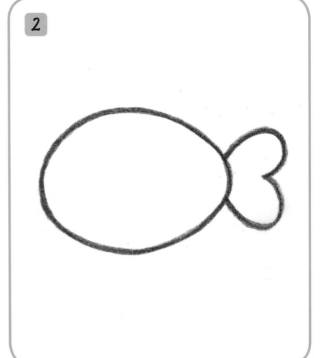

3

4

While Boomer is being scolded for the fish bowl disaster, Mew scampers upstairs, where she finds even more trouble. Mew tries to squeeze her paw through the bars of Squawk's cage! When Boomer hears the parakeet call for help, he runs in to chase Mew away. So only Boomer is there to blame when Mrs. Bailey comes to the ruffled bird's rescue. "BOO-MER!"

Draw Squawk the parakeet!

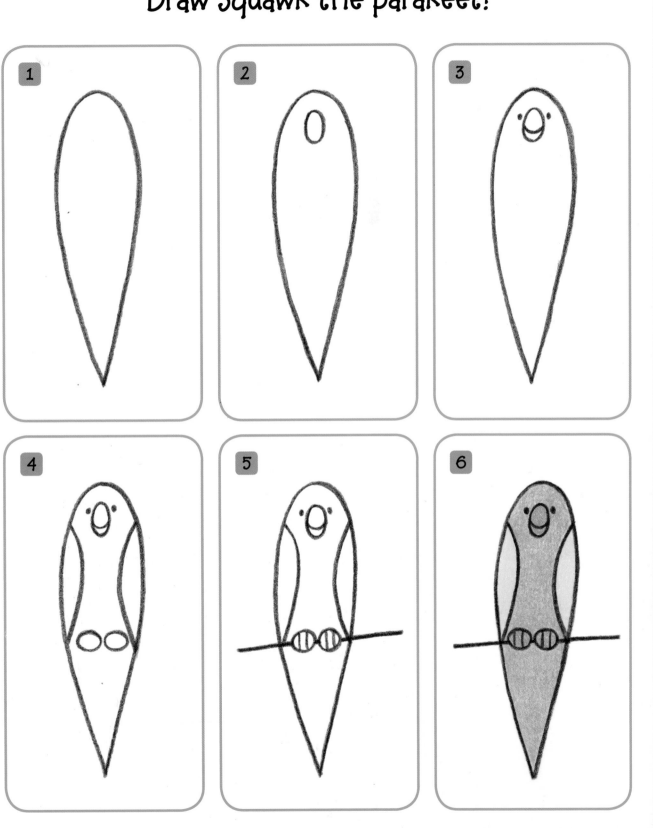

To keep Boomer out of trouble, the Baileys send him to the backyard. But what does he find just outside the door? Mew, again—and this time she is climbing the bunny hutch! In an effort to save his friend Whiskers, Boomer makes a dash for Mew. But she bounds off, and the bunny hutch comes tumbling down. When the Baileys find Boomer with Whiskers, you can imagine what they think! "BOO-MER!"

Draw Whiskers the bunny!

1

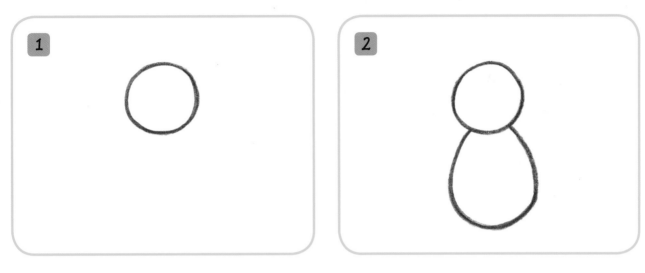

2

3

4

5

6

Boomer seems to be causing so much trouble that the Baileys decide to put him in the laundry room for a "time out." Boomer sighs. At least Iggy the iguana is there to keep him company. Or Iggy would have been there, if he hadn't slithered out the door when Boomer entered. Once Mr. Bailey finds Iggy in the bathtub, he blames Boomer. "BOO-MER!"

Draw Iggy the iguana!

1

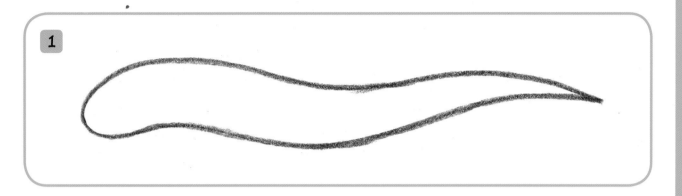

2

3

4

Mr. Bailey sends Boomer back outside. There, Boomer spots Houdini the tortoise. Houdini is finally coming out of hibernation, but he is struggling to climb out of the hole where he slept all winter. Boomer offers to help. But Mrs. Bailey doesn't quite understand the circumstances when she sees Boomer digging in the garden. "BOO-MER!"

Draw Houdini the tortoise!

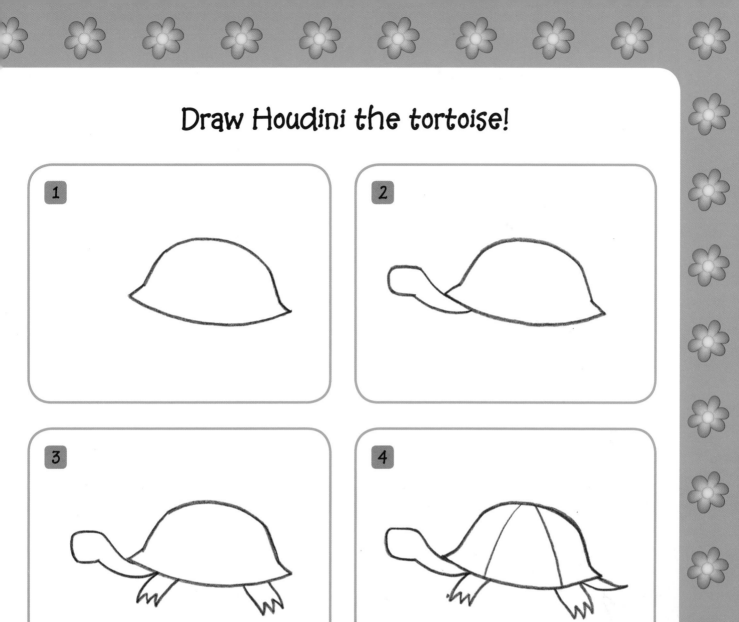

"I'm sorry, Boomer," says Mrs. Bailey, "but I'm going to have to tie you up to keep you out of trouble." Mrs. Bailey ties Boomer's leash to a tree in the corner of the yard. So when Boomer spots Mew chasing Crackers, the family duck, all he can do is bark in alarm. "BOO-MER!" yells Mrs. Bailey, "Stop making so much noise!" Of course, she blames Boomer.

Draw Crackers the duck!

1
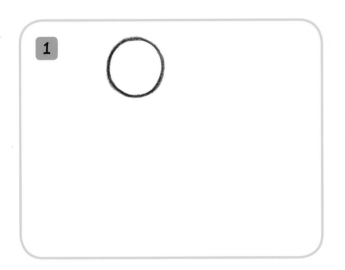

2
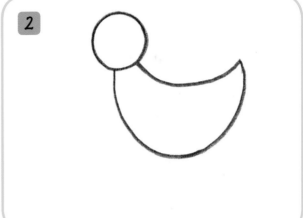

3

4

5

6

Boomer is frustrated that he can't keep an
eye on things, especially while Mew is on
the loose! Thankfully, Mr. Bailey comes out
to the yard. But Mr. Bailey doesn't unleash
Boomer. Instead, he ties up Hamlet, the
pot-bellied pig. Mr. Bailey grumbles about
muddy smudges on the carpet, forgetting
that it was Mew that chased Crackers
through the mud. Poor Hamlet!

Draw Hamlet the pot-bellied pig!

1

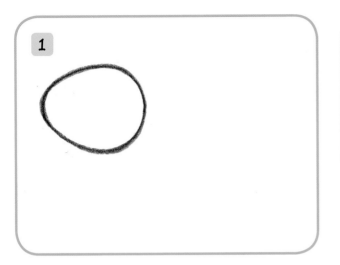

2

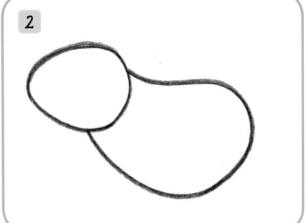

3

4

5

6

Boomer is surprised that the blame for the mud hasn't fallen on him! He is even more surprised when Bandit, the family ferret, comes scurrying out of the house with Mrs. Bailey hot on his heels. Bandit darts past the tree, but Mrs. Bailey stops there. "Boomer!" gasps Mrs. Bailey, "I could really use your help catching Bandit!"

Draw Bandit the ferret!

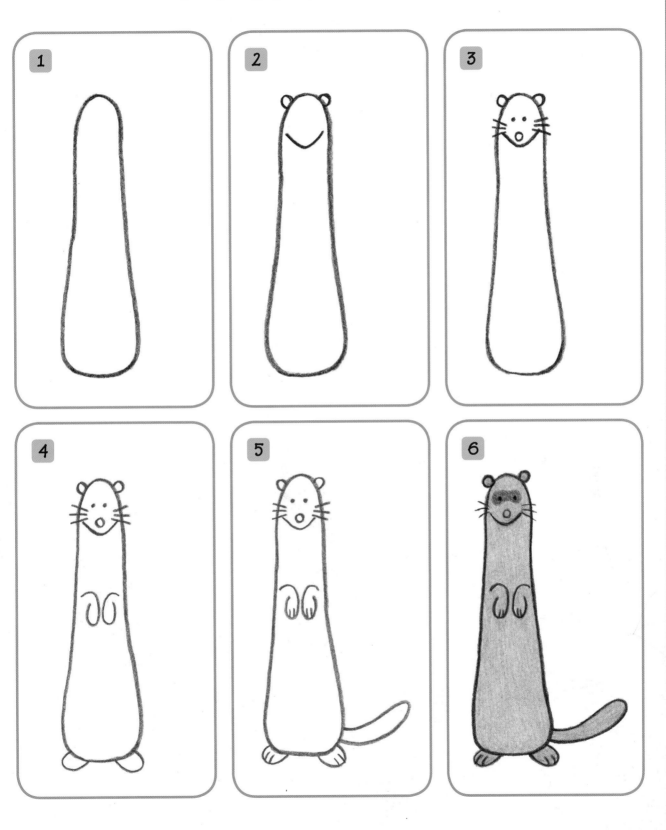

When Mrs. Bailey releases Boomer, he races inside to the hamster cage, where Dizzy is running on her wheel. Sure enough, Bandit dives for cover behind the cage—but Boomer quickly catches the ferret by the scruff of the neck, without interrupting Dizzy's daily exercise. Boomer receives a big hug and a pat from Mrs. Bailey. "Boomer," she says, "what would we ever do without you?"

Draw Dizzy the hamster!

1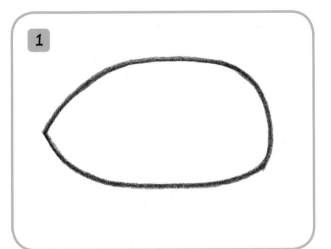

2

3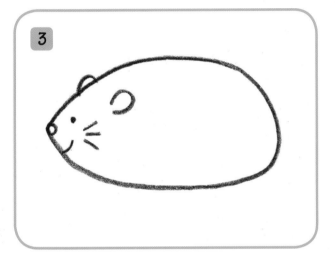

4

5

6

The end.